Praise for *Th*

The Currency Paradigm is a life-altering way of seeing beyond the lens of money. This new way helped me to expand into looking at energy, space, and time.

Gail Warner,
MA, MFT, author of
Weaving Myself Awake

The Currency Paradigm transforms the work of leaders. I can't imagine starting a project without asking how time, space, energy, and money will impact the endeavor.

Laura D.,
Nonprofit Leader, Fundraiser, and Woodworker

Hillary Augustine weaves together words, experience, and soul. She questions in a truly remarkable fashion; with a fierce gentleness that allows her readers to move at their own pace, and in their own way, all the while being guided by a master. Augustine is an articulate, soulful voice in a realm that is so often devoid of what really matters—both for the individual and for the collective.

Natalie Bryant Rizzieri,
author of *Muddy Mysticism: The Sacred Tethers of Body, Earth and Everyday*

I was sleepwalking through life and this book helped me wake up! This framework also supported me to locate important life currencies by finding creative ways to align them with the money currency. This book has shifted the way I see myself so that my decisions come from a deeper sense of self-love.

Matt Inman,
LPC, Psychotherapist

The Currency Paradigm—Time, Money, Energy, and Space—speaks deeply to me as an artist and creative-brained human. In the spaces where I usually shut down and clam up around money issues, these four currencies offer different portals to view, enter, and engage with my financial realities, with room left for creativity and intuition.

Brodie Peterson,
Multimedia Artist

Hillary's book is excellent. She has combined her educational degrees and directed the writing toward her clients' needs. She has kept it interesting by inserting her past jobs and travels. Good job!

Dad

Through sharing her story and the stories of others, Hillary opened my eyes to a new way of thinking about money—one that integrates soul and heart into money as a tool that serves in helping me live my most peaceful life *now* while also dreaming about my future. As a financial advisor, Hillary's work helped me connect what I feel with what I know.

Danielle Burton,
Financial Advisor

I read through the book on my deck—utilizing my Space Currency! It is very helpful to discover that my NorthStar currency is time. I tend to be very conscious about how long events will last. I also love to plan my calendar, making sure I don't schedule too much in a block of time.

Gary Vandenbos,
Retired USAF, CMSgt

This book opened my eyes on how I live my life. I learned how to express something I have always known, the value of energy and space. The concept of four currencies helped me communicate how I make decisions which to the outsider does not seem logical.

Dina Diab,
Strategy Consultant at The Big 4

The Currency Paradigm provides a useful framework for understanding the emotions surrounding all four currencies. Amidst a backdrop of intense emotions, priorities, morals, and values—it's never just about the money. Our behaviors are passed down from generation to generation, often taking center stage. Identifying and valuing all the currencies provides a shared language to guide emotionally charged conversations about how to "spend" these valuable resources.

Meagan M. Hyde,
MS, LMFT

THE
CURRENCY
PARADIGM

*A New Way to Exist
for the Empath, the Executive,
and the Edgewalker*

HILLARY AUGUSTINE

Cover Design: Asha Hossain Design LLC
Images under license: Shutterstock.com and iStock.com
Currency Symbols: Bronwyn Simons Enterprises
Photography: Talitha Bullock
Grammar Editor: John Olivares Espinoza
Developmental Editor and Book Midwife: Fen Druadìn
Publishing Strategist: Kory Kirby

Library of Congress Control Number: 2022915782

ISBN 979-8-986-82160-3 (paperback)
ISBN 979-8-986-82161-0 (ebook)

Hillary Augustine LLC books are available at special discounts for bulk purchase,
sales promotions, fundraising, and educational needs. Special books or book
excerpts can also be created to fit specific needs. For details and permission
requests, email: hillary@hillaryaugustine.com

Dedication

Writing a book illuminates the supportive
and connective fabric of my life.
A few special people are highlighted below, but
(of course) this list is far from exhaustive.
Thank you to multiple friends, clients, and family
for contributing to this creative work.

The next sentence has more gratitude than my limited
words are able to express. A special, heart-felt thanks to John
Olivares Espinoza for his editorial eye and to Fen Druadìn
for their book midwifery, attunement, and compassion. The
book you hold would *not* be in this form without them.

To Mom and Dad

You were my first incubation station for growing my
wings, testing systems, and generating ideas! Thank you
for raising a question asker. Also—to my brother—I know
you are proud of your sister even if you will *never* admit
my brilliance in public (said with a wink and a smile!)
I love you all.

To Mike

Thank you for being my Aquarius Flight Companion.
Lift Off!

To My Friends Across the Years

You know who you are because we connect frequently.
You've also heard about this book *over
and over and over and over* again!

Gratefulness Abounds!

These pre-readers jumped into the manuscript when
it was raw, mostly unedited, and full of wild hope.
Laura D.
Mike Vandenbos
Dr. Lynne Ellis-Gray
Jennifer Dawn
Brodie Peterson
Kayce Stevens Hughlett
Rich Ashburn
Ronna Detrick

TABLE OF CONTENTS

PREFACE

This is the beginning of the book, but it is actually the last section I completed.

Like sprinkles on top of a cupcake, I am thrilled to be at this stage in the writing process.

As I sit with my candle lit in the wee hours of the morning before the first sunlight cracks across the horizon, I am left with this question:

"Why did I write this book?"

Writing a book has been a long walk and an enlightening journey.

I have traveled across the United States and lived in Mexico, taking the contents with me while working with my evolving ideas. I sought the wisdom of different places, called upon friends, worked with energy practitioners, received bodywork, and interacted with my clients' suggestions to help me express what I most wanted to say. I have also been supported and loved by my companion across the years, who has been living The Currency Paradigm with me, day-by-day and breath-by-breath as I laugh and cry.

There have been times when I believed this book was done only to enter a long pause. These pauses were invitations to hear a client's perfectly expressed idea or to listen to nature's quiet whispers. In these moments, I was invited to discern what *might* want to join the page.

I now see that I wrote this book and offer my work because it is my highest expression of hope and love in a world that is harsh and lonely to the dreamers and the edgewalkers.

This book is written for me:

- The me that doesn't fit inside small boxes or within narrowly defined norms;
- The me I was finding along the way;
- The me I was leaving behind;
- The future of me.

Because of my roots of unbelonging within larger structures and systems, this book also doubles down on my commitment to support the expression and the cultivation of *new* imagination and *new* worlds for people who don't historically find themselves at home inside traditional frameworks. Name the structure—religious, financial, medical, educational, and vocational—I've probably questioned or have a story that has squeezed me out or made it too painful to stay inside tight, normative walls.

It makes sense that my gifts, my healing, and my pain are the eternal flame of my work, right? As I connect and work with people who also don't fit, I've found a space to exist. This space is heaven on earth for me.

This book is also written for you:

- The you that doesn't fit;
- The you that is growing and evolving;
- The you that is ready to imagine new ways and fresh worlds;
- The future of you.

How is this book organized?

This book is written with two distinct narrative voices and several sections.

One voice is the storyteller who invites you to enter the imaginative world of a little girl who grew up to be a bean counter.

The other voice is the teacher who introduces you to The Currency Paradigm with descriptions of each currency to understand the inner workings of the model.

At the end of this book, you will also find an invitation to The Currency Paradigm website. The website is a place where I have created downloadable worksheets with practices and thought-provoking questions to help you apply The Currency Paradigm Principles.

How do you read this book?

A conversation I had with a friend inspired this section. She said, "I wish there were half-books in the world!" Her desire comes from her rapid-fire intellect and her quick cycling energy which would love to read only half a book, apply what she learned, and be done.

Of course, she *can* do this.

Right?

It *is* possible to read half a book, get what you need and return later.

Yes, we know she *could* read in this way.

We can all read a book or live as we'd like, but do we *really* feel supported to read (or to live) differently? In our desire to live authentically, can we access our personal power, but also feel the vulnerability of living at odds with "normal"' or common expressions of life?

How many of us actually consider how we'd like to read through a book?

Or, on a bigger scale, how we'd *prefer* to live our life?

How many of us don't start a book because we feel it's too long; or, we don't have enough time; or we feel that reading *just* one page isn't enough or a half-finished book is a task left undone.

My friend's brilliant statement sparked me to write, "Read this book with permission to enter, leave, and return as you wish!" Whether you read half the book or a couple pages, give yourself the permission to say you are done.

Maybe you will discover a new growth edge within yourself? Perhaps, how you read *this* book becomes an expression of how you want to live *this* life. Woven throughout this book is the invitation to access your imagination and freedom, becoming an expanded version of *yourself.*

Enjoy!

ONCE UPON A TIME...

Once upon a time there was a vibrant little girl, who grew up to be a bean counter.

She took her role as a bean counter very seriously. She knew it was important to know how many beans there were and how the beans were being used. She knew somebody had to do this job, and she wanted to do it well. But, there was something missing.

She longed to count in a way that meant something.

She wanted to feel inspired and connected when she counted beans. Oh, how she loved when her friends' eyes glowed brightly, listening to her talk about the deeper meaning in the bean patterns!

She also wanted her bean counting to inspire the lives of others who exhibited vulnerability because they had experienced grief, loneliness, and the hardest parts of being human.

Unfortunately, she did not feel joy or connection in the bean counting world.

In fact, when she counted beans, the world grew dull and dim.

The other bean counters also lived in a dim world. They did not laugh, or cry, or share their struggles, though she could feel their vulnerable emotions. When she looked into their eyes, she noticed they *only* focused on the beans which limited their ability to see the range of beautiful colors and multidimensional options.

She named this world *Monocurrency* because its people existed in only *one* way. The Monocurrency World instructed her to count but never to feel. This split between counting and feeling was the first principle in *The Monocurrency Paradigm Guidebook*–a dusty book that upheld ancient instructions for monolife. This paradigm expected her to bring *only* her head, never her heart, to bean counting.

Although it did not feel right to her, she followed the instructions because she was young and wanted to belong.

She silently agreed to live among the Monocurrency People. She, like all those around her, swore to disconnect her feelings from her counting.

Time went on.

While she lived and worked in The Monocurrency World, the vibrant girl grew into a young woman who didn't see or feel a single spark of joy or hope. The only conversation between any of the bean counting people was about their beans.

- Were there more or less beans than last month?
- Did they owe anyone any beans?
- How many beans would they make this month?
- How many beans would they need to survive?

As the bean counting people asked these questions, the young woman began to realize something strange. Among the shiny, organized spreadsheets of counted beans, devoid of life and vitality, she began to identify her own nervousness and frailty and recognized these vulnerable feelings in others. She began to see what everyone had been trained to ignore—scattered papers and faces red with shame.

Even though they had all been taught to count, not to feel, she began to realize that they *did* continue to feel. Their illusions fooled them into believing their emotions had no connection to their beans and that their feelings were invalid.

She longed to give them so much more, *anything more*.

She began to see that perhaps there was another way.

Perhaps beans could come alive. Perhaps if planted, nurtured, and guided, beans could be both friend and companion. She began to live what she knew—beans could be vessels of strength, strong enough to shatter layers of shame—vibrant enough to resource one's life and the lives of many others—especially if they were watered and tended in favorable conditions.

Her understanding and passion grew stronger, but still, she felt odd and misunderstood. She journeyed through life—holding her secret knowledge close, cherishing it protectively like all do who aren't sure where they fit in, who feel afraid that their knowing might be misunderstood, who worry that they are too much, who sense they'll be seen as dangerous for daring to speak up, tip the scales, or tell their truth.

She put the beans of conscious calculation—her magical power—into a tightly sealed jar and stored them away.

She continued to find her own meaning with friends and healers who gave her space to uniquely exist, but something inside felt lonely, missing, and disconnected. Here, among the healers, she noticed that they avoided talking about their beans. Afraid that if they did, they would lose the magic of connection and freedom.

She wanted everyone to know what she knew about beans. They needed her and *her* bean counting ways.

Even more, the beans themselves wanted to be free, to be spread, to be planted! In her mind's eye—and in her heart— she saw beans as a portal to crack open new imagination and reshape lives.

The beans didn't need to be done away with! They needed to be shared in the ways that *she* knew and understood!

She couldn't hide her gift anymore. Longing bubbled up in her like champagne in a shaken bottle. Her *knowings* became more powerful than her fear. She knew she needed to spread her bean counting magic.

She became braver. She invited people to tell their bean counting stories. She asked about their numbers. She translated their words about decimals and commas into stories that were full of trauma, tears, celebration, pain, societal pressure, and even joy. As she listened, she felt life flow through her— head to toe. She began to let her heart speak while her mind calculated costs, envisioned opportunities, and reimagined hope.

More and more stories bubbled forth. Oh, how she loved hearing them. But, slowly and sadly, she began to realize that The Monocurrency World could not contain her fullness. She couldn't stay there, trying her best to translate The Monocurrency People's head-language with her heart-language.

The gap was too wide.

One day she made a promise to herself: she *would* share her gifts—as she had been secretly doing. She knew that stepping more fully into her powers meant that she would have to leave The Monocurrency World, where everything reinforced the split between head and heart. She would have to step into the gap and discover a new way of being.

And she did.

This young woman stepped into the void. She discovered new directions and clarity. She found a new integrated world, and, having found it, wanted others to join her. To help people find their way to this new place, she created The Magic Compass, a cosmic tool to guide them toward a fuller way of being.

This new world lived by a new paradigm, one where people could acknowledge their feelings *and* count their beans.

Beans and breath could coexist; bean counters and healers could converse; head and heart were both at home. She felt safe and alive. Others did, as well.

And now, magical beans could sprout and grow and live.

The Beginning…

Meet
The Bean Counter

I am the bean counter who escaped the illusion of The Mono-currency Paradigm where a single currency is acknowledged and discussed: money. In this one-dimensional approach, people are guided toward a dull and dim existence, focusing their attention one direction, disconnecting their head knowledge and their heart language as they count their beans.

In the gap between numbers and hearts, I discovered The Currency Paradigm—*A Guidance System and a New Way to Exist based on four individual, yet interwoven currencies.*

Let us continue!

"Talk about your money. Swallow your emotions."

Most of us would rather talk about the weather or something inconsequential than dive into conversations about money, finances, or bank accounts. Years of business experience and conversations have taught me how to traverse this harsh, yet intriguing landscape. Like the others who went before me, my financial degree fostered a dualistic, "calculate *first* and feel *second*" sort of reality. I learned that if I wanted to work in this realm, then I must forget pieces of my humanity to help everyone else forget theirs too.

Actually, the script goes more like this: "Don't feel at all. If emotions bubble up while talking about money, swallow them."

In the money world, our empathetic feelings are often viewed as incompetent and unnecessary.

I discovered that linear options and calculated answers are common solutions modeled in this world, but these answers dismiss people's pain, uncertainty, wildness, potential, and dreams.

Yet, across the years, I have met with hundreds of brave souls willing to take the plunge into the murky depths of their money stories while also experiencing new imagination.

These brave people hire me to help them cultivate inner and outer growth as they observe and learn how their life currencies fit into their greater lives.

These aren't just business leaders, savvy entrepreneurs and finance-oriented people. These are courageous healing practitioners, edgewalkers, and waymakers. These are people who ask the question, "What if?"

- What if there is **more** to money conversations?
- What if there is a better **way** to step into and navigate financial realms?
- What if there are innovative ways for finances to flow?

THE SPLIT

As I've journeyed through life, I have worried about a financial system that both modeled and required an emotionless space, shutting down significant factors to personal progress by cutting off hard feelings and unbridled hope. I have been concerned that the most shame-filled, vulnerable, and fearful parts of people's existence was not being understood and heard—really heard— in conversations about money. I have also been unsettled about financial practitioners who were trained to offer industry truths detached from their own feelings in a sterile, industrialized approach.

On the flip side, in the face of financial considerations, healing practitioners *and* money-oriented people alike have often become paralyzed and indecisive. Name the group–shamans, entrepreneurs, therapists, nurses, doctors, artists, yoga instructors, energy healers, executives, lawyers, astrologists, and pastors–I've witnessed the split between head and heart.

As you can see, the gaps between people who seek money help and the professionals who offer that help are many.

This split doesn't sit well with me.

> "Splitting (also called black-and-white or all-or-nothing thinking) is the failure in a person's thinking to bring together the dichotomy of both positive and negative qualities of the self and others into a cohesive, realistic whole."
>
> *from* "Splitting (psychology)"

Sweaty Palms and Red Faces

Perhaps all this sounds familiar to you?

You long to guide your finances with head and heart, but you've been in offices and across tables where money conversations felt tight and constrained, leading to a split and a gap between your mental intelligence and your mysterious, internal wisdom. As you calculate and measure, you feel your body seize up, short circuit, or split off from your bigger knowing. You feel "competing parts" of your humanness tighten up *even though* you intuitively know the benefit of calculation and measurement. The tears, sweaty palms, embarrassment, blotchy, red face, and rapid heartbeat communicate the underlying pain and tightness as you open up to discuss your financial past, present, and future.

Perhaps, you've visited with financial experts, bought all the accounting packages, tried the budgets, and checked off (or know about) the prescribed "list" of financial do's and don'ts—only to be left with too many calculations and big questions. What is forgotten is heart-felt vision.

Or perhaps you find yourself in a different dilemma.

You easily dive into financial calculations. In fact, you love them. You naturally see and calculate in numbers. However, in the process of counting, you lose your dreams and desires or the ability to experience relational connection to your whole life. Strict financial calculations flatten your experience and pummel you with societal guidelines about how your monetary landscape *should* or *could* be managed.

At this point, you may be wondering why so many people reside in a place where feelings and calculations struggle to coexist. There is a reason behind this place, this void, and this gap. It's called *Hallucinatory Capacity.*

HALLUCINATORY CAPACITY

Hallucinatory Capacity is the phenomenon or experience that refers to the human ability to ignore the existence of anything that an authority figure believes does not exist. Cross cultural studies by Blurton Jones "found in many hundreds of cases, all over the world, that [children] would point toward an object that [they] could see, and that, apparently, the mother couldn't see. And the child would keep pointing and pointing…trying to get some response [from his mother]" (Chilton par. 10). Restated another way, if the parent figure did not acknowledge the object, and thereby legitimize the child's experience, the child would unconsciously eliminate what they saw.

Hallucinatory Capacity invites the brain to eliminate new forms of possibility and imagination, deny creative solutions, and perpetuate a realm of limited options.

Whatever the parent legitimizes *is* the child's experience. Other options are eliminated so thoroughly that the child only sees limited solutions.

Unconscious elimination is exactly what happens in financial conversations. A "parent figure" or authority says, "This is how you should calculate your finances to be responsible." Or, "This is the money path that fits your societal norm." Or, "Don't worry about your finances, it will all work out."

This top down, outside-of-your-authority structure happens in childhood and continues throughout life.

Think about when you started to question what you believed and instead adopted what authority structures dictated.

As a result of systematic disbelief in yourself, perhaps you became stuck in your tracks, unable to entertain fresh realities. The other options that you might otherwise see or envision became invisible to you. Maybe a hallucinatory cloud enveloped you. Maybe you felt irrational or even stupid for what you saw and felt before the world swooped in to shrink your bigger, more authentic experience.

As people around you continued to test your perception, you might have felt the fog thickening. Perhaps you received prescriptive, institutionalized and formulaic options while judgments and common money rules created illusions.

In this vulnerable place of illusion and confusion, you didn't know what to believe, who to trust, what to say, and which way to go.

But...

- What if you aren't alone?
- What if there is a place where the cloudiness and fog is recognized and discussed?
- What if others are lost in this emotionless space of haze and disconnect, too?
- What if there is an entirely different way?

There is a way out!

PREPARATION FOR
THE JOURNEY

The etymology of the word *currency* originates from the Latin word *currere*, which means "to run." As we move forward, pay attention to the fresh insights that bubble forth as you consider your life as an electrical current or imagine your existence like a flowing river. Also, notice what happens to your body as you tap into your imagination or as you seek new and upgraded currency flow.

This book invites you to reimagine your entire existence outside the hallucinatory fog by acknowledging and valuing **four** essential currencies in The Currency Paradigm: Time, Money, Energy and Space. When all four currencies are acknowledged, they foster an integrated life, rich with imagination, potential, and meaning.

Let's set the stage to inspire all your currencies to flow!

As we imagine meaningful directions for your life, I invite you to dedicate this moment as a **new beginning**—a fresh start.

Dedicating—or ritualizing—deepens our experience. To dedicate means we mark, we set apart a moment to affirm our connection to whatever it is we are doing, bringing more of ourselves to the process.

As we move forward, perhaps you would like to:

- Light a candle;
- Prepare a nourishing meal;
- Pray, chant, invoke your personal Source or Spirit—whatever feels right to you;
- Go outside barefoot and feel your connection to the natural world;
- Prepare your favorite pot of tea;
- Build a fire;
- Talk to nature, animals, and humans;
- Walk among the trees.

As you read this book, reference these new vocabulary words. I hope these ideas and concepts illuminate your imagination!

CURRENCY PARADIGM VOCABULARY

The Monocurrency Paradigm: A Guidance System that recognizes only *one* currency, Money.

The Moneycurrency Paradigm Guidebook: A dusty book that upholds ancient instructions for monolife.

The Currency Paradigm: A Guidance System and a new way to exist that ascribes value to *four* individual, yet interwoven currencies: Time, Money, Energy, and Space.

Currency Bank: A place that holds Time, Money, Energy and Space deposits and withdrawals. Just like an actual bank account, the currencies ebb and flow in relationship to life choices. Every day you make currency deposits and currency withdrawals which constantly impacts your balances.

Currency Blocker: Any person, place, or thing that stands in the way of your North Star Currency.

Companion Currency Capacity: This phenomenon occurs when money is tended, observed, and guided across time. There is a companion or regenerative energy that builds with money when it is acknowledged as a relational currency working alongside the other currencies. In this way, money, like a person, has the capacity to give, resource, and come alongside (companion or accompany) the other currencies.

North Star Currency: Your most precious and valuable currency. This is the currency you guide, protect, and gravitate toward because you love how it makes you feel.

The Magic Compass: A supernatural, cosmic tool full of multidirectional possibilities. The four directions are the four currencies—Time, Money, Energy, and Space.

Golden Equation: An equation that includes a Quantifiable Currency (e.g., Energy and Space) and a Qualitative Currency (e.g., Money and Time). The Golden Equation invites dialectical wisdom—truth in *seeming* opposites—to summon forth greater currency understanding and insight.

Currency Poverty: The depletion or lack of any currency. When a currency is expended, it is like writing a bad check against time or against energy. In essence, you keep trying to use the currency after it is gone so the rest of your currency life "pays" for it. You bounce the currency—like a bad check—when you ignore its signals.

A CURRENCY BLESSING

As we explore The Currency Paradigm, I hope you feel a softening in your body where all forms of wisdom and truth flow multi-directionally. I hope you trust what you see and feel the wisdom of your experiences threading together. I hope you tap into your pulsing wholeness above the layer of hallucinatory fog. I hope you feel the sun warming your face, the wind at your back, the flowing water of your fluid being, and the ground beneath your feet, supported and enveloped with love and light.

The famous author, intellectual, and cultural critic, the late bell hooks, said it best:

> "To be truly visionary we have to root our imagination in our concrete reality while simultaneously imagining possibilities beyond that reality."

Let us proceed.

WHAT IS A PARADIGM?

A paradigm is a model or way of looking at something. In The Monocurrency World, beans have to be counted and bean counters have to count them. To be successful, bean counters are encouraged to detach from their emotions—no other thing should have an influence on their bean counting. That's their paradigm, their model, their value system. The bean counters create and continue their paradigm through learning and behaving in line with *The Monocurrency Paradigm Guidebook*–a dusty book that upholds ancient instructions for monolife. They abide by their paradigm by collectively affirming emotionless counting and continual rejection of any wild ideas that threatens their bean counting traditions.

If we dig deeper, we can also see how a paradigm is maintained through Hallucinatory Capacity, where the child eliminates or accepts what is important to their model based on what their authority figure acknowledges or eliminates. In essence, a paradigm is the ingrained patterning that is learned, observed, shared, and reinforced by a collective group of people; therefore, we can describe a paradigm as:

- a model or pattern for something that may be copied;
- a theory or a group of ideas about how something should be done, made, or thought about.

Phil Jones, Chief Executive and Founder of Excitant, a management consultancy, explains a paradigm shift like this:

> So, when people talk about *experiencing a paradigm shift*, they are saying that a fundamental part of their model of the world, as they see it, has changed and their model no longer works. It is time to change or adapt the model. They may have to make a fundamental change to their beliefs and working assumptions about how they operate. For them, the paradigm shift is in *the implication of the change*, as much as the original source of the change. If a change does not cause a model to break, or to be reappraised, it is not a paradigm shift. (par. 19)

Why Is It Time for a Paradigm Shift?

"If you are a poet, you will see clearly
that there is a cloud floating in this sheet
of paper. Without a cloud, there will be
no rain; without rain, the trees cannot
grow; and without trees, we cannot make
paper." (95)

Thich Nhat Hanh

Thich Nhat Hanh invites us to consider everything in the context of interconnectedness where, for example, the paper we use is connected all the way back to the clouds in the sky.

We exist in a time in human history where outdated, one-dimensional models are unraveling. This great unraveling offers an opportunity to see the power of intersection and stand in awe of the mystery of new possibilities.

In the realm of money, we have been taught that money is not connected to the rest of our wellbeing or to other currencies. As we leave these outdated, one-dimensional models behind, we make room for new understandings to emerge.

The current money model, or The Monocurrency Paradigm, is broken because it conveys that money stands alone outside of an interconnected, natural arc, separated from our humanness. We tend to feed separation myths by attaching the worst human emotions to money: anger, greed, shame, embarrassment, and resentment.

No wonder it is SO hard to guide our relationship to money in imaginative and positive ways. We are living a split reality in a divided world!

There is another way.

Like many, I was going down the Monocurrency Path. But my internal alarm sensed there had to be more integrated ways to understand money!

ONCE UPON A TIME IS MY REAL-LIFE STORY.

At an early age, I was educated in The Monocurrency World. I completed a Master's in Accounting (MAcc) which led to preparing tax returns and assisting the CPA partners with high-end divorce cases.

My accounting position placed me at financial tables with varying levels of wealth in complicated, heated emotional environments. I was good at it. But, because I had extensive personal counseling in my teens and early twenties (read: I had a lot of therapy), I constantly felt that something was missing in the gap between numbers and emotions.

My therapy sessions were focused on building a person—me—from the inside out. In contrast, my financial training felt institutionalized, disembodied, and formulaic.

In these two *seemingly* opposite worlds of accounting and counseling, I felt that we were creating incomplete human maps and hallucinatory ways to exist. We were using maps that only accounted for one direction.

The fog wouldn't let us see other directions, or if we did see, we immediately needed to unsee those possibilities to comfortably exist in a one-dimensional Monocurrency Paradigm. Sure, the map *might* lead to more beans in the pot if we could follow it, but how could we follow it faithfully when other directions were arising: rains from the west, sun from the south, and winds in the east kept calling to us?

It was as if we lived in a world where there was only north, but no east, west, or south.

Within The Monocurrency World, I felt the pulsing desire to listen and acknowledge these other directions, to honor my multidimensional reality.

I kept thinking there must be more than one direction!

My search for other directions!

My search for other directions and deeper integration led me to pursue another master's degree. This time, in something that is widely considered the very *opposite* of a career in the financial world—a degree in counseling!

It wasn't an easy decision. While working for the CPA firm, I was also deeply involved in therapy through individual counseling and support groups. My program director made a completely ludicrous suggestion. He asked me if I would *consider* the counseling world as a profession—a place to guide my future.

Wait? Was he suggesting that I leave the lucrative profession of accounting, where I had already invested years of my life for something entirely different? Was I really supposed to start again?

After laughing—yes—really, laughing, I began to feel the *raw truth* of his invitation sink into my life. These coexisting activities—CPA firm by day and therapy world by night—fed both my head and heart. What if there was a way to integrate the two?

Looking back now, I recognize his curiosity as an invitation toward a new paradigm. He was acknowledging a world outside my narrow, Monocurrency understanding. He witnessed my vibrancy during support groups and in therapeutic circles, *spaces* that ignited my *energy* and in a divine way aligned my gifts.

I felt the currencies of space and energy begin to dance with the *Accounting Hillary* who focused on time and money. My program director's absurd sounding idea to pursue a counseling degree **after** completing a Master's in Accounting opened up a new life pathway.

Laughing was my unedited response as I assimilated the raw, uncomfortable feelings mixed with pure excitement. My old paradigm was crumbling, and I knew it. His "terrible" suggestion was actually a beautiful acknowledgement of what brings me alive.

"But, the way my life's been going, that would be a terrible idea."
"A terrible idea. Don't you love those?"
Under the Tuscan Sun (2003)

It was a *terrible idea* because to change career courses meant losing my momentum, or so I thought. A very real chasm existed in the face of switching careers.

I was trained that you don't give up what you've accomplished in the business world. You keep climbing the rungs.

You rise. You follow the carrots of money and bonuses and job status. You make a mark.

There were many invisible and visible costs to consider.

The Visible Choices.
The Gap.

Exchange the financial world for a profession in counseling?
Really?
Master's in Accounting:
Good Salary.
Yearly Bonus.
Stable Future.
Known Path.
My mind asked all sorts of questions
of the imminent life shift.
"Were there signing bonuses in the mental health world?"
"A free laptop?"
"Free drinks and happy hours?"
"Partner status?"

I don't think so.

I could see the extensive list of what could happen if I moved away from the financial world. But, I had also experienced what could be gained in the counseling world. There was no turning back.

In making this life decision, I was beginning to understand, and even live into, the value of currencies beyond money. I was *also* valuing the capacity of money by listening to what it wanted to fund and how it wanted to flow.

One day she made a promise to herself: she would share her gifts—as she had been secretly doing all along. She knew that stepping more fully into her powers meant that she would have to leave The Monocurrency World, where everything reinforced the split between head and heart. She would have to step into the gap and discover a new way of being.

And she did.

Switching Directions

I was faced with my own growth edge.

Would I turn back?

Continue to build my financial roots and stable path?

Or transplant myself into the next unknown place... choosing wild uncertainty.

I did it. I switched paths. I stepped into the void and began my journey towards a Master's in Counseling (MA).

I was literally changing directions, following the rains of the West (Seattle) and leaving the sun of the South (Florida) to seek out new places of integration.

My move from the South to the West acknowledged a life map with many directions. The split between my head and heart began to soften as I broke free from one direction to seek another direction. My new path turned on a faucet of energy and vibrancy.

The fog began to dissipate.
I was finding my way!

This young woman stepped into the void. She discovered new directions and clarity. She found a new integrated world, and, having found it, wanted others to join her.

I was integrating and upgrading my existence.

I was discovering a creative path, a map between worlds.

I was exploring a new way, based on four currencies, not just one.

I was living The Currency Paradigm.

The Currency Paradigm recognizes four individual, yet interwoven currencies, which operate like the four directions.

Time, Money, Energy, and Space.

The Currency Paradigm is rooted in one simple concept:

If we want to experience a greater sense of wholeness and meaning, we must acknowledge total currency flow.

Do you sense fresh possibilities as you see your life from a multi-currency perspective?

Perhaps you are already sensing a currency block or a currency that needs tending?

Or, on the flip side, maybe you are well aware of a currency that is flowing and vibrant?

Let's explore your intuitive promptings!

THE CURRENCY PARADIGM

To begin our currency learning, we will discuss and highlight each currency to elevate our understanding. We will explore Time, Money, Energy, and Space to acknowledge their value and learn how each currency, when experienced in its highest form of expression, enriches our lives.

The Currency Paradigm lifts the hallucinatory fog, opens new doors, and expands our awareness of other opportunities.

Here we go!

- Let's observe the common ways we use and guide each currency;
- Let's acknowledge all the currencies to highlight their unique and individual values;
- Let's consider the highest expression for each currency;
- Let's imagine how the currencies flow when we view them through an integrated paradigm, connected to the rest of our lives.

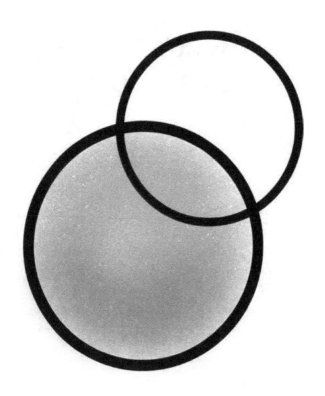

TIME

What is Time?

Let's observe how time is used and guided in our everyday existence.

Time is often heard in the tick-tock of the clock, seen in the second hand continuously moving, or the numbers digitally changing on a computer or laptop. We count time and see its passage in the movement of numbers.

> Time passes in seconds, minutes, days,
> weeks, months and years.
> 60 seconds, 24 hours, 365 days.

In our jobs...

Most jobs orbit time. Jobs are described as full-time or part-time. Contract or freelance work is often built around time; this is the cost or quote for a given amount of time. In many industries, clocks are punched or time is billed. For example, attorneys and accountants track minutes to convert time to money. Appointments are made according to time.

In our education and our religions...

From a young age, school kids realize that a ringing bell indicates the passage of time. Also, in villages across the world, the sound of bells from a church or minarets signify hourly prayer or remind worshippers of special ceremonies.

In our entertainment...

Sports are also built around time; the basketball is thrown down the court one last time and the buzzer ends the game. The last toss of the football spirals across the field as the timer hits zero and the fans for the team with the ball hope for one last touchdown while the opposing team revisits all the bad calls that should have frozen time.

Time is very important in these scenarios. It is the main indicator of measurement, productivity, and the difference between winning or losing a game.

In childhood and human development...

There are other ways to experience the movement of time. We witness it when children go from newborn to high schooler almost overnight. Older people often talk about time moving in the "blink of an eye." We also see the passage of time in an aging animal's gray whiskers and time advancing on our natural bodies as wrinkles form in the face.

The ancient passages of time are also known through nature as seasons shift and the moon continues her cycle: new moon, quarter moon, half moon, and illuminating full moon.

Time moves and flows...

- in bells and alarms;
- in nature and its seasons and cycles;
- in the acknowledgment of the aging process;
- in moon cycles.

In The Monocurrency Paradigm, time is alone, separated from the other currencies.

Time is counted, checked off, billable, expendable, and limited. Meaning, there is no bigger purpose in time except to track it and use it. Time stays separate from our lives as an object to contain our schedule. It can also be a judgmental authority and hard taskmaster, reminding us if we are "ahead" or "behind" on a timeline while comparing our activities to other people's accomplishments. In its limited expression, time is a one-dimensional currency, efficiently managed and scheduled.

What is an integrated model of Time?

In an **integrated** model, time connects to cycles and seasons. For example, people often say, "When the timing feels right, I will _____." In this sentence, internal *feelings of time* guide their external experience. People convert the concept of time into a cyclical-based, intuitive understanding to access something larger and beyond the linear view of time. It is also common for people to reference an *internal clock,* recognizing the pulsing of time toward *this* or *that* opportunity. They may not know the reason why "time is ticking," but they speak about a timing premonition, an invisible and mysterious force that beats internally.

At its highest expression, time becomes timing. It is a **Connector Currency** that helps us reflect on our **past,** tune into our **present**, and envision the **future.** On occasion, timing cycles are known, planned, and directed. Other timing moments are mysterious, an invisible force beckoning us onward.

Major life changes activate new timelines. I've heard numerous stories where people sell everything or leave their job because they surpassed the age of a parent who died unexpectedly. Or, they leave a marriage or long-time partnership, have a baby, or get a new job. Life and death along with beginnings and endings activate timing thresholds.

My experience of Time as a Connector Currency.

When I shifted career paths, I released my original, linear timeline which focused on climbing the professional accounting ladder. My understanding of time evolved and became more fluid. Also, by releasing a sense of *time control,* I invited more options for my career. In this experience of time, the intuitiveness of timing became my guide instead of the linear-tracking of *mentally focused, calculated, laddered-time.* In essence, I left the indoctrinated timetable and replaced it with a broader sense of *timing*!

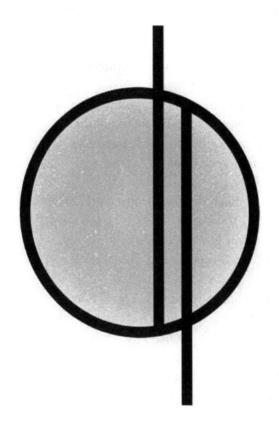

MONEY

What is Money?

Let's observe how money is used and guided in our everyday existence.

Money is commonly recognized as the *only* currency.

Money is quantifiable. It has a shared language. It is unique in the way it gets moved, utilized, and valued.

It also has a measuring system.

It passes back and forth in movements called transactions to symbolize value exchange.

People use terms like savings, investing, spending, budgeting, and expenses to speak about money.

Because money has a shared language, it also has repeatable and common questions:

- How much does *this* or *that* cost? Dollars and cents.
- Can I afford *this*?
- Should I be paid more?
- Is *this* too expensive or too cheap?

In The Monocurrency Paradigm, money is considered alone. Money is separate from the other currencies.

When money is alone, it is *only* used and seen as transactional.

In its more limited expression, there is no greater purpose or reason for money besides counting it, spending it, saving it or investing it.

The business world says, "Time is money." The creative world *often* says, "Money is energy." In these perspectives, people are *trying* to eliminate the complexity of money by making it synonymous with time or energy.

Yes, time *does* convert to money as we see in many professions and money *does* give us energy if it flows in the directions we desire, but money doesn't become another currency.

By conflating money with another currency like energy, it loses its unique identity and wipes out its inherent essence. *Money is money.* It seeks to be individual, distinctive, *and* yet interwoven with the other currencies as we learn to place it in an integrated model.

What is an integrated model of Money?

In an **integrated** model, money is a **Companion Currency** that reveals our fears, exposes our wounds, and resources our dreams. As a companion, money acts as a **mirror** which reflects where we ascribe value. Money is both relational and transactional.

My experience of Money as a Companion Currency.

When I shifted from accounting to counseling, I guided money toward therapeutic realms where I felt spaciousness and energy. Money accompanied my life by moving toward places that felt valuable (counseling) and away from places that felt dried up or untimely (accounting). In the years leading up to my career shift, I felt prompted to save money for some unknown future shift so I could access money's resourcing capacity. Money was building **Companion Currency Capacity** as it grew in its sacred container (i.e., my savings account) until I was ready to spend it.

As money ran in new directions, I was faced with my fears of scarcity, my hopes for the future, and my temporary disorientation. Fear and disorientation, alongside new dreams and aspirations are all indicators of a paradigm shift. I was breaking free from The Monocurrency Paradigm.

Acting as a mirror, money exposed places of growth and supported my overall currency existence. Money operated at its highest expression because it functioned from its intended role as a mirror and a companion. In essence, money served as a relational force, not *just* a transactional exchange.

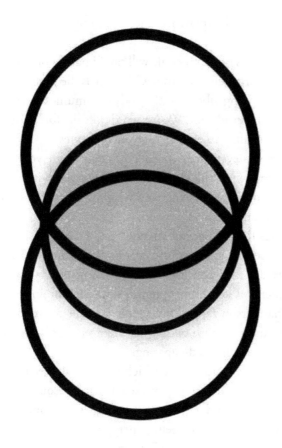

ENERGY

What is Energy?

Let's observe how energy is used and guided in our everyday existence.

We feel and experience energy through its presence or absence.

If energy is present people will say, "I have a lot of energy." Or, "My energy felt good today." Energy is the pinging, panging, and popping vibes that the body communicates and radiates from the inside out. We use words like life force, vibrancy, joy, or adrenaline to express high energy zones.

Have you ever experienced a moment where your energy was flowing, vital, and expansive? Or, have you witnessed the running, bouncing, playing, and wiggling of a child or puppy with unending vitality?

This is the presence of energy.

On the flip side, we use words like depressed or overwhelmed as descriptors for low energy, or no energy scenarios.

If energy is absent, people will say, "I felt drained today." Or, "That person zapped my energy." People reference burning the candle at both ends when their energy is low or the "flame" of their life is dissipating.

Unlike time and money which we quantify, energy is not acknowledged as a currency or exchangeable resource because it is experienced and felt, not counted. In The Monocurrency World we get 'close' to seeing energy as a currency by stating that our energy is "spent." Energy is expendable if we are tired or drained, but beyond that general description, energy is ignored.

Sure, we have medical devices and calorie counters like Fitbits to give us a quantifiable understanding of how much energy we burn. But, these devices aren't a communal tracking tool, or a way to exchange energy; instead, they are personalized measurement devices.

Anytime a currency isn't shared or measured, it's less likely to be valued.

The expression of energy is limited when it is stuck and neglected.

Stagnant energy does not run, flow, and pulse through our lives.

When energy is not acknowledged as a currency, it wilts like a plant without water or sunlight.

What is an integrated model of Energy?

In an **integrated model**, energy is acknowledged as an **Attunement Currency** that is meant to be listened to, valued, discussed, and felt. When we attune to our energy—which is *also* our life force—we feel a greater alignment, resonance, and expansion. High expression, energetic people have a skip in their step and a twinkle in their eye. You can feel their essence and vitality when they enter your life.

Energy offers us messages about our inner and outer worlds. It pulses, rests during dormancy, protects what is important, activates our dreams, and aligns our lives. Energy is the force that births new realities into being or highlights the ending of cycles when it ceases to pulse and flow. It starts, stops, and maintains many daily activities and bodily functions.

My experience of Energy as an Attunement Currency.

If I had ignored the invitation to seek another career path, I would have missed my vibrant energy barometer which flew off the charts when I considered leaving accounting. My insides screamed, "Yes! Yes! Follow *that* path!" Energy was guiding the opening toward my counseling future while also temporarily rerouting the energetic flow away from my accounting career.

At its highest expression, energy served as my internal barometer and **Attunement Currency** to protect and activate my future path. Ancient fears arose as my old paradigm crumbled and my new world began. My fears wanted to shut down this *ridiculous idea*, ditch the new plan, and stop the vibrant flow. I'm thankful energy protected me, keeping me attuned to the wholeness and rightness of my shift.

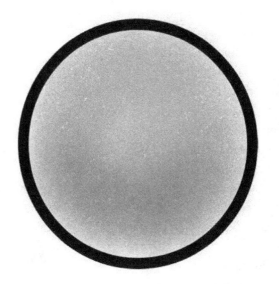

SPACE

What is Space?

Let's observe how space is used and guided in our everyday existence.

Because space is the most mysterious and multifaceted of all currencies, it is the most ignored; therefore, I'll take a bit more room to explore its nuances, its power, and its three distinct dimensions.

Space is internal, external, and spiritual or soulful.

Internally, we often describe space in terms of feelings inside the body.

For example, think about what it feels like to have constricted or expanded airways.

Take a deep breath. Feel into it. What happens to your chest when you breathe in and breathe out? Do you feel expansion or constriction or a bit of both? Is your breath shallow and blocked or free and flowing? This is one way to gauge spaciousness in your body.

Internal space is cultivated or accessed in sacred moments. These moments can be found in many contexts.

For some people, internal space is discovered:

- During long nature walks;
- Sitting around fire circles;
- Movement;
- Traveling to various places;
- Enjoying silence on a meditation cushion;
- Engaging in conversations with an attuned friend.

As you reflect upon these scenarios, do you feel your body open spatially? What happens as you imagine long walks in the woods or interacting with spacious people who extend permission (space) to be yourself?

Another way to consider space is **external.** For example, if I shift an item in my physical space (e.g., home, office, car), I feel expanded; if I declutter my space, it feels spacious; if I move spaces, I feel lighter and more vibrant.

We also feel space in the **spiritual or soulful** realm.

In a metaphysical way, this aspect of space is beyond the body and outside rational understanding. It is transcendent. In this realm, people describe the "hairs on their neck" standing up because of a *knowing* or *mysterious presence* that cycles through their body from another dimension or space.

For instance, premonition, answered prayers, and undeniable signs and symbols cycle through our lives from this *other* space. This is the aspect of space where we aim our yearnings to connect our earthly bodies to heavenly realms. The soulful aspect of space is also where deep meaning guides people's lives in moments of life, death, tragedy, unexpected surprises, trauma, and mystery.

Also, just like energy, space is not commonly measured or shared in our everyday lives. It is worth repeating, anytime a currency isn't shared or measured, it is less likely to be valued.

Space is *often* only acknowledged in the physical realm. For example, this is the space or the house where I live. It is the currency that is most ignored or filled up (i.e., "I have no space."). It resides in thick *hallucinatory fog, invisible to the seeing world.*

In its limited expression, there is no space. Think claustrophobia.

A life with no space is like living without breath. There is no inhale or exhale.

If spatial constriction had a sound, it would be a gasp or a screech.

Imagine listening to music without any measures or sections. The spaces—or measures—in a musical composition create beauty and invite the listener to settle in, enjoy, and flow with the sound. If the notes are clumped together, without digestible sections, we would hear chaotic, overwhelming noise. We would want to cover our ears and close our eyes. This is what a life without space feels like: chaotic, crazy making, smashed together, and vibrationally abrasive.

Or, imagine reading a page with no margins or spaces between words. The spaces of a book allow the reader to pause, take in the structure, and feel the rhythm of the story. Without spaces, we would see a string of letters, not meaningful phrases and sentences.

What is an integrated model of Space?

In an **integrated model**, space is a container and holder of all that is present and all that is becoming in the internal, physical, and metaphysical realms. Space is a powerful, multidimensional currency that holds infinite possibilities.

Space is the **Container Currency.** When space is empty and not always filled it has the potential to summon forth new life and welcome fresh vision by making room for a wide range of experiences.

My experience of Space as a Container Currency.

Long before my career shift, I sought more space to exist. Seeing a counselor in my teens and twenties, facilitating and participating in weekly support groups, and seeking out the most spacious people were a few of my *life signals* that the

Space Currency *really* mattered. A counseling degree, which focused on people's stories, made sense because it was a wide and spacious career that allowed for an unlimited range of experiences and possibilities.

I can still feel myself take a deep breath as I reflect upon my career shift memory. The pursuit of counseling softened the constriction in life and gave me room to explore, grow, and exhale.

I felt spacious.

Space was holding me and I was feeling held in a life path that symbolized infinite possibilities.

MAGIC COMPASS + NORTH STAR CURRENCY

**Remember The Magic Compass
she summoned forth...**

This young woman stepped into the void. She discovered new directions and clarity. She found a new integrated world, and, having found it, wanted others to join her. To help people find their way to this new place, she created The Magic Compass, a cosmic tool to guide them toward a fuller way of being.

Now that we've discussed each currency, I want to introduce you to a playful, cosmic tool I call The Magic Compass.

Begin by familiarizing yourself with your compass.

Your supernatural, cosmic tool, full of multidirectional possibilities!

Notice the four directions are the four currencies —Time, Money, Energy, and Space.

Notice that you may feel drawn to one currency more than other currencies.

When I made my first leap into the void, away from The Monocurrency World, I didn't have The Magic Compass. I had to summon it, craft it, and test it as I fell through the fog.

Without The Magic Compass, you risk being transported back to The Monocurrency World where head and heart disconnect and only one direction—or one currency—is seen and acknowledged.

During this transformational journey, it is very common to be pulled back by old, habitual ways. Bobbing in and out of foggy illusions is part of the traveling journey between old and new paradigms. Even though the fog is unsupportive, it is still familiar, and, as humans, we gravitate toward well-worn pathways.

I am honored to be the vessel by which The Magic Compass enters the world, to help others shift their lives with greater confidence.

Find your North Star Currency!

To begin using your Magic Compass, you will want to find your North Star Currency.

Notice that this compass doesn't *tell you* what currency is *your* north.

You set it.
You choose it.
You discover it.

This is a very important step to personalize and calibrate your compass so that it is in sync with your intuition.

Here are helpful prompts to identify your North Star Currency:

- Identify a significant moment or life memory when you felt *the most* aligned.
- Which currency felt the strongest?
- Which currency did you prioritize?
- Set this currency as your true north.

When you set *one currency* as your true north, you are acknowledging that any person, place, or thing that takes you off course or stands in the way of your North Star Currency is a **Currency Blocker**. You are also stating that your most precious and valuable currency must be protected so that other currencies align and orbit your North Star Currency.

> **Currency Blocker:** Any person, place, or thing that stands in the way of your North Star Currency.

In my story, we see *over and over again* that I was spending immense amounts of time, energy, and money to create more space. My natural gravitation toward space led me to identify my North Star Currency. For example, I began therapy in my teenage years, participated in support groups, and surrounded myself with people who valued the exploration of this vast, human experience called *Life*!

The other currencies are also important, but they aren't the currency I serve, cultivate, and constantly consider. I care SO much about spaciousness that I naturally seek spacious places and people. This also means that I resist *any* person, place, or thing that feels tight or constrained or attempts to define my life path or my values. In this way, the Space

Currency—the infinite holder of possibilities—keeps showing up as my most valuable, North Star Currency.

The content of this book arises from my **internal space**—my body's wisdom—onto the page. I also prioritize and move into various **physical spaces** to support my writing. I've traveled to various cities, countries, and other creative spaces to complete the book you are reading.

Even now, I am completing this manuscript from Mexico City—a country and a city that accesses my heart energy. Mexico connects to the **metaphysical and mysterious** nature of my heart and soul. The land is unexplainably supportive and deeply felt.

In these ways, I am attuning to the multiple dimensions of the Space Currency: internal, physical, and metaphysical.

Check. Check. Check!

This book arises from the highest, intersectional vibration of the Space Currency because it is born out of the protection and guidance of my North Star Currency.

When I prioritize SPACE, the other currencies - TIME, ENERGY, and MONEY - realign to help guide, cultivate, and protect my life's infinite possibilities. I hope you feel spatial alignment through these pages, inviting your expansiveness!

What currency are you always feeding, stoking and cultivating?

At this point, you may have a clear picture of your North Star Currency.

Great!

Calibrate your compass.

Set your true north.

If you have difficulty picking one currency, no problem. It can take some time to achieve the right calibration.

Remember, a sense of natural ease or longing for more inner agency from a specific currency is an important distinction when choosing a North Star Currency. A primary or North Star Currency makes you feel good when it is prioritized and when it is operating in sync with your desires. As your mind and heart gravitate toward your primary currency, you *want* to keep drawing from its power because you LOVE how it makes you feel when it is aligned.

My North Star Currency was identified by what I *naturally gravitated* toward—space and spaciousness.

To help you gain North Star Currency discernment, let's explore commonly expressed characteristics of people who naturally gravitate toward each currency. Remember, in the spirit of half-books, if you feel like you have identified your North Star Currency, then you may skip the next section if you wish.

The North Star Currency of Time
What are the characteristics
of a Time Person?

In an **integrated** model, time connects to cycles and seasons. At its highest expression, time becomes timing. It is a **Connector Currency** that helps us reflect on our **past,** tune into our **present**, and envision the **future.** On occasion, timing cycles are known, planned, and directed. Other timing moments are mysterious, an invisible force beckoning us onward.

People who are good at time or timing are naturally grounded and attuned to the rightness of timing. In their highest expression, time people *naturally and effortlessly* pay attention to earth-based schedules. They often sense larger shifts like closing or opening a business, moving, having a baby, adopting a child, or beginning and ending a relationship.

If guiding time makes you feel tight or constrained, it is not your primary currency. Instead, it is your adaptive currency. For example, you might be forced to be a "time person" because of life circumstances, but not because it's natural or enjoyable to you. We all adapt to schedules, but for Time People the flow of time through their body and in their lives **is innate, natural, and produces a feeling of groundedness.** Time People don't feel constrained as they move through life with an awareness of time.

They also don't pack their schedules like an energy person often does, but instead they intuitively grasp what can be scheduled and completed according to the time allotted. People who are naturally good at sensing "right timing" guide their best lives by listening to their internal timing clock while syncing it to their earth-based existence.

If you are attending a party with a Time Person, they will easefully state, "I need to go now," because they are past their bedtime, or their babysitter's time is running out, or they are sensing a squeeze in their schedule. Time People actively participate in **shaping their time currency to elevate their overall currency flow** by scheduling their lives based on their connection to their internal and external (digital) clock.

Time People **speak** in time by saying things like: "There's no more time or we have five minutes remaining." With daily schedule choices or in company meetings, Time People pay attention to realistic timelines for project deliverables. They are good at knowing how long something will take.

Time People feel pulled to honor the container of time by saying, "We are out of time or over time. We need to end this meeting." They know when they are "overstaying" their personal or business engagements—often without checking a clock—because they have a wonderful sense of time being used up or time being wasted.

Time People hold the natural ability of helping themselves and others contain and complete scheduled activities. Time People also have mysterious premonitions about the unfolding of earth-based timing. They access intuition, groundedness, and expansion through the navigation of time.

Summary

Time People sense what is happening through the connection of the past, the present, and the future. Because time is their North Star Currency, they often feel ignored or neglected if people are continually late or if they don't get enough quality time. Unacknowledged tardiness or a rushed life (no time) ignores their most **precious currency.** Time People also despise getting blamed or assigned to projects that have tight timelines because this squeezes their primary currency. Time People avoid choosing life situations that give their *time power* over to others because they derive their natural strength from time management or guidance, the source that wields their mysterious wisdom.

The North Star Currency of Money
What are the characteristics
of a Money Person?

In an **integrated** model, money is a **Companion Currency** that reveals our fears, exposes our wounds, and resources our dreams. As a companion, money acts as a **mirror** which reflects where we ascribe value. Money is both relational and transactional.

Money People comfortably move around money. Their movements *might* look effortless or magical to people from the outside, but often Money People are thoughtfully attuning and planning while calculating financial implications.

Money People also don't have to hold onto money or amass it—that's *generally* not their overall driver. Instead, they allow money to come and go. Attach and detach cycles are a significant part of their guidance system, life lessons, and strategy.

Money People *might* have worries and fears, but they perceive these concerns as growth edges and a playground for their human and financial development. As they navigate financial cycles, they use money to learn about themselves. They ride and track *wavelike* experiences to deepen their personal understanding of risk and reward as they "play" with their financial portfolio. Money is a long-term game with relational life lessons and challenges. In many ways, Money People guide their money like an artistic painting—with every financial move or stroke of their money brush—they learn how the *new colors* or money fluctuations impact their financial picture.

Money People often seek advanced financial training or mentoring to understand the intricacies of money language, financial forecasting, and investment portfolio strategy. They have a deep desire to *be good with money or to understand its principles* to make it work for them. They study their risk profiles and tap into their life flow based on what money can do or not do. As they grow and expand, they are often found sharing their insights and their resources with others.

A Money Person knows their numbers in a different way than most people. They cultivate their human development through the lines of financial awareness, aptitude, and financial resiliency. They *seem* magical with money and its rhythms, but behind the scenes they are consistently observing their daily cash flow fluctuations and long-term financial horizon.

Summary

Money People are often labeled unempathetic or unemotional because they naturally live in a mental headspace. They are overlooked for their practical and rational ideas because they have difficulty bridging their intelligence with what they see in the present or predict in the future. They often need other people to help explain the *money map* inside their head. Even if they are predicting a strong financial profit or money excess—good news that people *should* want to know—their insights need a translator because they speak in data which is hard for many people to process or understand. Society tends to listen to Money People through the filter of personal judgment because financial conversations hold shame and stigma, a very high hurdle for Money People to clear when communicating their wisdom.

The North Star Currency of Energy
What are the characteristics
of an Energy Person?

In an **integrated model**, energy is acknowledged as an **Attunement Currency** that is meant to be listened to, valued, discussed, and felt. When we attune to our energy—which is *also* our life force—we feel a greater alignment, resonance, and expansion. High expression, energetic people have a skip in their step and a twinkle in their eye. You can feel their essence and vitality when they enter your life.

Energy People are often the life of the party. They naturally draw others to themselves because they change the vibration of a whole room. However, they also have the potential to exhaust people who aren't naturally wired toward regenerative energy.

For Energy People, *regenerative* is a keyword. Energy People are *very* sensitive to any person, place, or thing that contains or controls their energy. To most people, it seems that Energy People have unlimited or **more** energy than the average human, but if we take a closer look, the Energy Person actually regenerates as they move through life—moving in and out of environments with high energy or expansive energy. In a high vibrational state, Energy People prioritize and flow with their energy. They rest and rejuvenate when they feel their energy wax and wane.

Sometimes Energy People lose track of their most precious currency, spending it to the point of exhaustion and depletion. This volatile energy cycle spikes adrenaline which fuels the Energy Person in the short term but creates long-term energy draining scenarios.

Energy People often enjoy high adrenaline work environments like busy restaurants, bustling hair salons, volatile tech startups, emergency medical careers, or other pressure-filled, deadline-oriented jobs that fuel and rely on compacted, elevated, and fluctuating energy. They often start companies or accept positions that reward them for their energy—commission gigs or equity stakes are great compensation models. This ties their pulsing energy directly to their performance.

I joke about the fact that *often* Energy People have a technology device with *at least* one cracked screen. Meaning, their laptop, phone, or iPad is either mangled, cracked, or dented. The technology warranty folks make a lot of money from Energy People because their devices are forcefully impacted by their fast moving, sporadic, and quick-cycling energy.

Energy People speak and answer in energy. If a Time Person texts, "Are you able to meet at 2:00 p.m. to walk?," the Energy Person *might* answer at 1:59 p.m., with a "YES, sounds good." The Energy Person received the text, registered the request, and said "YES" in their mind and heart without actually communicating to the Time Person. The Energy Person also believes the walk can *still* happen—*as if* the Time Person kept that window of time open to shift quickly for the Energy Person. Instead, the Energy Person didn't consider the transitional time necessary to make the walk happen and the high probability that the Time Person *probably* prioritized their Time Currency, making plans without them.

Let's imagine a likely "end" to this scenario. I can envision the Time Person enjoying their daily, 2:00 p.m. walk while the Energy Person talks on their cracked-screen phone and commits to four other spontaneous activities!

An attuned Energy Person is regenerative, bringing their high vibration to everything they touch and see!

Summary

Energy People do not like to be held back. They feel suffocated if their movements are controlled. A statement like, "You are stepping on my airpipe or my life oxygen," is a sentence to express the constriction an Energy Person feels if they are forced to guide their energy against their will. They don't want their sporadic, pulsing energy contained because it *is* what keeps them alive.

The North Star Currency of Space
What are the characteristics
of a Space Person?

AHHHH Space, *my* North Star Currency.

> In an **integrated model**, space is a **Container Currency** and holder of all that is present and all that is becoming in the internal, physical, and metaphysical realms. Space is a powerful, multidimensional currency that holds infinite possibilities.

A Space Person cares a lot about their physical environment. They also attune to how spacious they feel in their surroundings which includes people, places, animals, and nature.

For example, I wrote this section of the book at 4:30 a.m. with coffee by my side, a quiet house, a settled universe, and a lit candle. Right before the sunrise, my ideas flood forth. My creative energy relies on space and spaciousness. I've come to learn that space is an important, life-giving currency because I know what it feels like to *not* have spaciousness. As I prioritize my Space Currency, I feel my body relax and greater wisdom arise.

Space People naturally speak in spatial terms. They use language with room, meaning they pick words with airy, nebulous qualities because they carve out space for new visions, open concepts, and fresh ideas.

They make sure their calendars aren't filled up, allowing for pockets of time to accommodate what might want to join the schedule as the week and month unfolds. For example, Space People pick what fills their lives based on how spacious it feels. This means their schedule could look full, but upon closer inspection, it is filled with items that aren't constrictive to the Space Person. Often activities like planting a garden, redecorating a room, puttering around the house, cooking soup, taking a walk, or sitting in a meditation circle have a ritualistic or nurturing quality to them. The *busyness* of a spatial person's life is oriented toward expanding and creating greater spaciousness, not *just* filling the day with a list of items.

As I've become more attuned to my spatial needs, I've played with various levels of schedule flow and spatial transitions. I love to work from different countries and states, traveling here and there to feel the energy of the space that supports me. In this way, space and energy are always interacting, but I lead with spatial shifts in order to gravitate toward the energy of the land that draws me to it.

A spacious life is a big inhale and exhale!

Summary

Space People avoid anything that takes up or defines their space. On the flip side, they avoid narrowly defined people, places, or things because there is a Space Currency risk of squashing mystery and cutting off curiosity. They value immense room and space to allow personal truths to arise. In essence, strict definitions *about anything* give the Space Currency Person an instant rash!

They are often misunderstood or overlooked when they speak about divine nudges or mysterious truths because they appear spacey and hard to follow for those seeking quick solutions, solid facts, and bullet points. They value spaciousness to work things out and create what hasn't been created, *yet*.

You are well on your way!
Explore your North Star Currency

Here are some more questions to guide your North Star Currency discernment:

- What currency feels most unaligned when it is absent?
- What currency do you miss when you don't have access to it?
- What currency feels grounded, putting you at ease when you guide and shape it?

Now that you have further knowledge about each currency, the different types of Currency People, and the strengths, tendencies, and growth potential of each currency, you are ready to pick and play with your North Star Currency.

As you explore a new relationship to your North Star Currency…

- Protect it.
- Guide it.
- Cultivate it.
- Talk about it with others.

How does it feel?

Do you feel more aligned when your North Star Currency is front and center, serving as your anchor and your guide?

Grab your Magic Compass.
Set your North Star Currency.
Enjoy your new insights!

GOLDEN EQUATION

Let's add more possibilities to currency exploration!

Finding your North Star Currency is the first step toward discovering your Golden Equation.

What is the Golden Equation?

The **Golden Equation** is found by blending one Quantifiable Currency (Time and Money) with one Qualitative Currency (Energy and Space).

The Golden Equation is built on the principles of dialectical wisdom. *Dialectical Wisdom* originates from blending *seemingly* opposite perspectives, ideas, or concepts to dissolve preconceived notions. When currencies are blended, they activate a synthesis zone which opens new perspectives and

> **Golden Equation:** An equation that includes a Quantifiable Currency (e.g., Time and Money) and a Qualitative Currency (e.g., Energy and Space). The Golden Equation invites dialectical wisdom—truth in *seeming* opposites—to summon forth greater currency understanding and insight.

catapults us beyond the hallucinatory fog. Black or white, all-or-nothing splits cannot exist when currencies are combined to release greater understanding!

The Golden Equation encourages us to ascribe value to our Energy and Space *in concert* with our Time and Money. In this equation, we do not ignore *any* of the currencies, feeling a unifying force throughout our whole selves. When we feel unified, we can operate in a fog free zone, above or outside of splits, ready to play with new blends, colors, and dimensions.

Let's find your Golden Equation!

*One Quantifiable Currency blended
with One Qualitative Currency*

Time and Money: Quantifiable Currencies

Time and Money are often discussed in quantifiable, number-oriented ways, such as, "I have $5.00 in my pocket" or "I am meeting her at 11:11 a.m." When a currency has a common language, it is used more frequently to describe life situations. Think about how often you refer to money in your daily existence or how you orient and plan your schedule around numerical time. It is very common to relate to life through the currencies of Time and Money.

Energy and Space: Qualitative Currencies

The currencies of **Energy and Space** have no common language. Even though energy is converted to calories, it isn't shared among people for exchange in the marketplace or to orient our collective existence. I don't share my calories with you or "schedule" with you based on my caloric intake, so it's an individual value system, not communal.

Therefore, it is easy to miss the inherent value and presence of energy and space. Energy and space come from an internal knowing, bodily response, or gut-level vibration. And, with space we also have the multi-layered reality of physical space, internal space, and metaphysical space. We know when a person "takes up our space" or "drains our energy," not because someone calculated it or quantified it for us, but because it is experienced.

We are now learning that the Quantifiable Currencies (Time and Money) must be considered with the Qualitative Currencies (Energy and Space). The Golden Equation recognizes the dialectal wisdom when quantifiable and measured currencies (Time and Money). coexist synergistically with intrinsic and intuitive currencies (Energy and Space).

The Golden Equation:
One Quantifiable Currency (Time or Money)
blended with
One Qualitative Currency (Energy or Space)

Discover your Golden Equation!

- What is your North Star Currency?
- Is it experienced/qualitative (Energy and Space) or measured/quantifiable (Time and Money)?

- If your North Star Currency is Energy or Space, then choose Time or Money as an *opposite currency* to explore.
- If your North Star Currency is Time or Money, choose Energy or Space as an *opposite currency* to explore.
- You will find your Golden Equation by blending your North Star Currency with an opposite currency.

As we've seen in my story, I was protecting and cultivating my North Star Space Currency. But I was also guiding another currency during my discernment process, overall growth, and healing: Money.

My journal notes were full of calculations, moving expenses, and future income ideas. I calculated the unknowns of my companion currency (Money) to attune to my upcoming coast-to-coast move. I projected future costs and cash flow, but I also felt waves of worry and fear because I did not want to run out of money. My calculations helped me honor my Companion Currency (Money), which had a lot to teach me. Money *wanted* to help me as I thoughtfully planned expenses and generated income ideas, but I did not know how my move would *actually* unfold. I calculated a good, aligned savings—based on what I thought I needed—then I acknowledged the fears and worries that arose as I moved toward my imminent life leap.

My mental chatter and anxiety wanted to attach all the heavy and hard feelings to my Money Currency, but as I unraveled my worries, I realized my uncomfortable emotions were rooted in my relationship to risk and leaping into the unknown. My anxiety was *actually* tied to breaking historical, personal, and societal money patterns. Even if I calculated a good *actual* savings number to accompany my move, the rocky emotions were still present. Money was teaching me to listen to it *and* attune to my body. Money also wanted to accompany and support my cross-country move!

Money was saying...

"Calculate and then jump!"

"Calculate and then trust!"

"Calculate and then I will help you, Hillary, to follow your pulsing energy toward a new space!"

The Money Currency was the Quantifiable Currency I was blending with my Qualitative Currency (Space) as I faithfully followed the rains of the West while leaving the sun of the South.

My Golden Equation

I now realize that anytime I'm faced with significant life shifts I consider my Space Currency *with* my Money Currency as I discern how to navigate life's many questions:

- What workshop will I teach?
- Where will I travel?
- Should I offer *that* person or organization my currency of time or money?
- Whom will I hire for *this* project?
- What kind of environment or person is best for me?
- Should I move offices or home locations?
- What coaching, or business, or healing services should I invest in?
- Where do I want to give or guide my Money Currency?

When I spend, save, or guide money to access space or spaciousness, I know I'm in my currency sweet spot because I'm considering my Golden Equation: Money and Space.

My Golden Equation helps me intersect, honor, and understand the depths of my complex humanity, because I'm activating dialectical wisdom where truth is found by combining *seemingly* opposite currencies: **Qualitative Currency (Space) and a Quantifiable Currency (Money).**

With my calibrated Magic Compass plus my Golden Equation, I lift above the fog, breaking free from The Monocurrency Paradigm.

CURRENCY STORIES

Working with The Currency Paradigm

The Currency Paradigm elevates our conversations by fostering greater understanding about our currency flow or lack thereof. Multidirectional currency solutions include and allow for human complexity while replacing the typical one-dimensional approach. With this new paradigm, the hallucinatory fog vanishes and infinite possibilities arise.

To see how this works, let's step into Currency Stories!

Amelia's Story

debt, money, and unhealthy relationships

Problem: Amelia wants to pay down debt, eliminate interest payments, and feel more financial ease.

Monocurrency Solution: With The Monocurrency Paradigm, a spreadsheet would typically be created to clearly and systematically itemize a debt paydown plan. Often, the assumption behind the spreadsheet is that it encapsulates a **good** roadmap for Amelia to "responsibly' and 'consistently" decrease her debt balances.

In The Currency Paradigm, we want to avoid a binary method of good vs. bad, and instead step into knowing that this is *one* of many approaches. Although a clearly itemized debt paydown plan is *one way* to review the numbers, it is not a holistic solution.

Simultaneously, we understand that in a Monocurrency Solution, *solely* based on managing, counting, and guiding money, we miss the bigger picture. In this solution, a Monocurrency fog exists to hide other approaches.

The danger of the Monocurrency approach is that Amelia feels judged and ashamed because the prescribed and formulaic plan does not fit her way of being. Also, this solution espouses a one-size-fits-all model, with a rinse and repeat methodology which misses the complexity of Amelia's situation.

Currency Solution: In The Currency Paradigm, money is a companion and a mirror, working with Time, Energy and Space.

Amelia arrives at a coffee shop to meet with a friend. She is attempting—again— to get on top of her debt. She is ready for the challenge but scared to speak about the weight and shame of her life in *actual* dollars and cents. She knows that reflecting on her money translates into painful reminders of a recent relationship breakup.

Her pain and embarrassment manifests in her flushed face, physical exhaustion, and trickling tears. Speaking about her financial situation to a friend is the hardest thing she has ever done. She is making the invisible weight (debt) visible by stating her money details. Amelia knows "what to do." Across the years, she's read and accumulated many financial books and combed through extensive blogs. From her many attempts, she has learned that one-size-fits-all financial principles will not be the answer to her debt reduction.

She's ready for something new.

Amelia has been focusing on growth and development for a consistent period of time through our financial consulting work blended with her ongoing therapy sessions. For several solid months, we have identified all the circumstances where Amelia gives away her currencies which spins a web of monetary indebtedness, but also creates other currency shortfalls, such as being short on time, energetically depleted, and spatially constricted.

Through our work with The Currency Paradigm, she begins to imagine her money as a companion and advocate. She envisions each dollar toward her debt as a psychic and energetic unwinding from a terrible relationship that left her with massive debt weight. The debt has an energetic core which keeps spinning her into shame-filled, self-sabotaging scenarios.

She works on crafting a debt reduction plan that activates her money to release psychic weight. She coordinates the pay-down plan with the 18-month anniversary of her breakup. In 18 months, she wants her money picture to show a tangible representation of her personal growth. **$0.00 debt** symbolizes a new line in the sand of her financial existence. Her internal mantra is, "No more relationships that leave her holding the weight of debt."

With the new plan, she activates the Time Currency by setting a clear 18-month goal to lift old, stuck energy and psychic weight. She helps unwind the Energy Currency by setting a new Life Intention to protect her future energy by *not* lending money she does not have. Amelia's New Intention reactivates her Energy Currency and allows her Money Currency to fund *her* life rather than being siphoned away toward other people's expenses. As Amelia guides her currencies, her debt decreases, her energy rebounds, and her spaciousness expands.

Amelia's Currency Solution

In her ideal Currency Plan, money is ready to be the best advocate. It saddles up to energy in a strong and powerful way. Money simultaneously reduces the debt while untangling past energetic blocks and repeated patterns where intimate relationships and debt are inextricably bound. Strategic timing is activated by linking debt pay off to her 18-month breakup anniversary. Every dollar guided toward her debt releases her bound up energy. She is beginning to envision a new, expansive future!

As Amelia continues to explore The Currency Paradigm, she discovers energy is her North Star Currency. She remembers all the life altering moments that naturally activate her energy: traveling, hanging out with supportive and encouraging people, and taking flying lessons to become a pilot.

Her coffee shop friend also reminds Amelia of all the ways she uses her energy! She enjoys coaching middle schoolers on weekends. Her energy also ignites with fresh ideas and participation in her executive leadership group. Her friend knows that when Amelia's energy is alive and pumping, she is unstoppable; therefore, refueling activities, like traveling and playing soccer, are top priorities in Amelia's currency solution.

Amelia is working with her Golden Equation, blending the power and relationship of money and energy to see what is possible! In her paydown plan, Amelia is excited to explore how her Golden Equation will keep her aligned and thriving.

This is a hopeful currency solution because it's integrated at multiple levels. It's also a sustainable path because all currencies are in their highest expression, supporting Amelia's new existence!

Skylar's Story

constriction, unhealthy habits, and trauma

Problem: Skylar wants to move to a new city, state, or country, but he believes it is too expensive.

Monocurrency Solution: With The Monocurrency Paradigm, Skylar would consider the financial implications of moving and calculate the expenses.

Typical financial considerations would include:

- How much does it cost to ship possessions?
- How much does it cost to rent or buy a house?
- How much does it cost to maintain his chosen lifestyle? (i.e., dining out, commuting, entertainment, etc.)
- What if Skylar loses his job because of this move? That's a huge financial cost!

All of these money-focused items are helpful considerations, but they don't highlight other costs buried in the hallucinatory fog. If Skylar *only* counts the financial implications, he will miss the greater dimensionality that is bound up in his desire to move and shift.

Currency Solution: In The Currency Paradigm, money is a companion and a mirror, working with Time, Energy and Space.

Skylar arrived in his home city nearly 20 years ago for a career shift. He heard about the job opportunities, the vibrant music scene, and the amazing restaurants. He loved many attributes of the city, but he faced challenges connecting with friends as the urban density and traffic increased.

He feels badly about his desire to move to another location because his job has amazing growth potential. Even though he can work remotely for extended periods of time, his networks, yearly bonuses, and future advancements are location dependent. His financial path is well laid out if he doesn't change anything.

However, his health is suffering. Recently, his loneliness and isolation have contributed to extra drinking and unhealthy, packaged food choices which have led to weight gain. His body and spirit show decreased energy. His soul feels barren and desolate, leaving him without a larger purpose or vision.

He desperately wants to move or at least travel, but his Money Currency fears pull everything into unalignment. His deepest fears consist of making less money or losing his job. He grew up poor and *never* wants to return to poverty. The scarcity he experienced throughout childhood is set deep in his bones.

As he considers future shifts, memories of his past flood in, halting imagination and dreaming. He breaks into a sweat. His somatic response reminds him of the fights his dad instigated with multiple bosses, resulting in perpetual job loss. Even thinking about voicing his request to move kicks up unemployment fears. He's stuck in either/or thinking, because any shift or stated desire automatically means Skylar will lose something—just like his dad who was continuously jobless.

Skylar knows he must look into his personal abyss to face his fears. He also knows that guiding money towards his move and speaking with his boss, is *just* the beginning of unraveling deep-seated trauma from scarcity and deprivation.

As he journeys with The Currency Paradigm, he's unsure how to identify his North Star Currency. He's always given away all his currencies, so he doesn't know what it's like to live without perpetual currency depletion and elimination. Skylar wonders if he has created another kind of **currency poverty**, swapping his past money poverty for constricted time, energy, and space depletion. Skylar senses he must cultivate and explore each currency to identify his North Star Currency and Golden Equation. There's more work to do, but where should he begin?

> **Currency Poverty:**
> The depletion or lack of any currency. When a currency is expended, it is like writing a bad check against time or against energy. In essence, you keep trying to use the currency after it is gone so the rest of your currency life "pays" for it. You bounce the currency—like a bad check—when you ignore its signals.

As he feels the extent of his currency deprivation, he has *one* hopeful spark and memory! He remembers a somatic healer that his friend suggested years ago. Maybe this practitioner can help him regain freedom and wholeness in his body. Maybe this is a good starting point for currency realignment?

He makes one of the most important Space Currency decisions of his life. He schedules a somatic healing appointment to focus on his body. His currencies are now flowing in a different direction!

Skylar's Currency Solution

In his ideal currency plan, Skylar envisions approaching his boss to request more time off while continuing to explore his healing.

He fears his time-off request might eliminate his annual bonus. Worse yet, what if he loses his job? At the same time, his current employment is one of the main contributors to his time poverty cycle and unhealthy lifestyle. He feels the bind from multiple directions.

He must do something!

His current job demands won't let him rest or unplug. The financial incentives to live near the headquarters bind him to a dense city and a lonely home.

Through The Currency Paradigm, Skylar starts to consider his energy and space along with his time and money. He takes a 360-degree assessment of all his currencies by reviewing and imagining how he can shift each currency into a better position.

He wonders, "Can his money be an advocate for funding healing practitioners to help explore his perpetual job loss fear?" He also wonders if his money flow will adjust to re-companion the life he *actually* desires. As Skylar works with the constriction of each currency, he begins to access a whole new currency horizon. This isn't an easy journey, but Skylar is gaining strength, paying attention to his body, and seeking support.

Eventually, Skylar gains the courage to step into a new life of travel and adventure, accessing his Space Currency *and* his Money Currency while breaking free from deep-seated, generational fear.

Phoebe and Seneca's Story

"Successful," but discontent existence

Problem: Phoebe, Seneca, and their family built the life they *thought* they wanted. After many years, they have a profitable business; however, they are feeling perpetually constricted and stressed.

Monocurrency Solution: In the Monocurrency Paradigm, they would consider a major life shift by reviewing the financial implications. They would financially assess the costs and benefits of various possibilities and focus on the responsible choices which *might* include staying on the current path to earn plenty of money.

Currency Solution: With The Currency Paradigm, they would consider all four currencies. How are they flowing, not flowing, constricted, or stressed? Consider how a life shift can help overall currency flow.

Phoebe and Seneca have built a busy life in a thriving city. They have a nice home and are "financially successful" according to some people's ideas of prosperity. But, they are unhappy and unhealthy.

Phoebe and Seneca are disoriented because they have attained Monocurrency Success that others look up to, but something is missing. As they begin to explore the flow of four currencies, they realize their currencies are stuck and constrained. In The Monocurrency Paradigm, they have a narrow perception of currency—only acknowledging financial implications—which limits their ability to feel expansive and imaginative.

Phoebe and Seneca want to have more power over their choices and also desire a life with time to breathe, rest, and shift into something new. After many conversations, they start dreaming about enjoying their time and increasing their energy in exchange for giving up money—for a season.

After many lengthy discussions and late-night deliberations, they decide to make a life- changing decision against incredibly aggressive and negative feedback from friends, family, clients, and employees.

They decide to "throw in the keys" on the life they have built and move to a new city. Only a handful of friends understand their decisions and desires. Without a multi-currency framework, Phoebe and Seneca don't know how to help their unsupportive friends envision new perspectives.

In an attempt to explain it to others, Phoebe and Seneca name their life shift, "Family Reboot 2.0." Then, through The Currency Paradigm, they find language to describe their journey between their old and new existence. They imagine and map out what it means to realign all currencies. The Currency Paradigm helps them legitimize their questions, decisions, and late-night deliberations. Everything clicks into place from there.

Phoebe and Seneca's Currency Solution

As they work through each currency, Phoebe and Seneca have an *Aha! moment.* They discover that their unhappiness originates from time, energy, and space deprivation. For years, there has been no extra money after paying bills, but even as savings grows, their fulfillment does not.

Meanwhile, they pay an incredible amount of money to restaurants and food delivery services because they are busy operating the family business. Little time at home means minimal home-cooked meals, prepared with love and spaciousness. Even though Seneca loves to cook, she consistently expends all her currencies. Nothing is left in her currency bank account for meal preparation.

With The Currency Paradigm, they realize they are not cultivating the currencies they value, such as allowing extra time and space for family fun and healthy meals.

Once they start to see their currency operating system, they *also* recognize The Monocurrency Paradigm in their friends' lives. They realize their friends react and live in a monolife, making more money, but ignoring the other currencies.

With currency language, their life-changing decision transforms from an "irrational, irresponsible" shift—as seen by others—to a thoughtfully debated, well-measured choice. They now use currency language as a way to show the motivations behind their move, which shifts negative or confused responses to, "You're my new hero" or "I wish I could do that."

They tell people they are freeing up space and time to enjoy their kids. They are downsizing their home and increasing their yard to access more nature. Not only will more outdoor space help their kids learn to garden, but it will allow them to run and play.

As Seneca and Phoebe begin to imagine options to replenish their depleted currencies, they also see how they can create their own currency reality rather than live within the stories they have been given or the stories they feel pressured to uphold. They now use The Currency Paradigm to guide what jobs to pursue, where to live, and where to spend their entertainment and restaurant dollars. They don't ignore any currencies by factoring in time, money, energy, and space equally.

Life Stories are Currency Opportunities!

The stories of Amelia, Skyler, Phoebe and Seneca are composites of the Empaths, Executives, and Edgewalkers that have found their way to my services.

I work with creative people. People whose lives are legitimized, valued, and make sense *only* with multidimensional solutions. These stories are commonly misdiagnosed and pre-packed as financial problems, which leads to narrowly defined and shame-based solutions.

**We don't have to live in the fog of
The Monocurrency Paradigm anymore.
Now we know, there are more
currencies and many directions!**

Our Magic Compass reminds us to stay faithful to our North Star Currency and our Golden Equation. We see and value the currencies of Time, Money, Energy, and Space equally. Job changes, life shifts, debt paydown strategies, moving possibilities, vocational dreams, relationship commitments, and investing options are transformed into universes of possibility with The Currency Paradigm.

Do other currencies exist?

Now that your imagination is primed, pulsed and open, you may be wondering if other currencies exist. This is like asking me if there are other habitable planets? I think it's possible and probable. Why not?!?

Here's how I think about the existence of other currencies.

I have been asked if concepts such as **love, companionship,** or **friendship** are currencies. I consider these concepts as expansive or constrictive in relationship to the other currencies. Here's an example of how *supportive* friendships influence Time, Money, Energy, and Space:

- My **Time Currency** is witnessed with long-term friendships who know about my history and remind me of significant life moments. Therefore, when we share memories, I become more aware of my past, present, and future (unfolding) timing cycles.
- My **Money Currency** feels less constrained when I experience companionship. Friends remind me of good, nurturing support. As I feel appreciated, I am simultaneously reminded to allow money to be like a good friend that *wants* to accompany and resource my life.
- My **Energy Currency** is ignited because I feel loved. My energy expands through good friendships because we uphold one another's dreams and desires.
- My **Space Currency** is cultivated and supported with kind, loving friendships that want me to grow, expand, and spread my wings.

Supportive concepts like love, companionship, and friendship are all **currencies expanders**. On the flip side, currencies are constricted when these relationships are toxic, unsupportive, or when judgment, jealousy, abandonment and neglect are present.

I invite you to consider the ways currencies expand or contract for you!

Along the way if you discover another currency, please tell me! The Currency Paradigm is a universe of unfolding possibilities.

I left the Monocurrency Paradigm!

...So can you!...

I had to journey into the split between my head and my heart to discover The Currency Paradigm. The integration of the split happened through valuing and acknowledging other currencies.

The Currency Paradigm answered the following significant questions:

- How could I bring more of myself to others?
  Answer: *By acknowledging and playing with four currencies, not just one!*

- Where could I express my full heart *while* calculating the monetary impact of life decisions?
  Answer: *The Currency Paradigm!*

- Where could I honor my financial discernment *while* following my intuition and heart tugs?
  Answer: *The Currency Paradigm!*

> *This new world lived by a new paradigm, one where people could acknowledge their feelings and count their beans. Beans and breath could coexist; bean counters and healers could converse; head and heart were both at home. She felt safe and alive. Others did, as well.*
>
> *And now, magical beans could sprout and grow and live.*

Life with The Currency Paradigm

The Currency Paradigm has taught me to guide and protect my North Star Currency while attuning to the infinite possibilities of my Golden Equation. I am gathering an extensive list of beautiful memories by working with all four currencies!

- **My work:** I blend accounting and counseling to offer an innovative approach to conversations about money, meaning, Executive Coaching, and Life Design. I also help people cultivate and grow their imaginations, which is the soil of their future dreams! My work is a lovely blend of head and heart with all the currencies acknowledged and valued.

- **My travels:** I have experienced many traveling adventures as I access my Golden Equation. I spend, save, and guide **money** to access **spacious people** and **places.** I often say, "Travel IS my therapy." One of my favorite traveling memories is walking the Camino de Santiago—the ancient Spanish Pilgrimage. Holy smokes! SPACE expanded. I have many memories from long, daily walks and deep conversations with Peregrinos—pilgrims on the path.

- **My best car purchase:** At the ripe, young age of sixteen I bought a Ford Festiva. I guided my companion currency (money) from my McDonald's job to purchase my **red, spacious, magic on wheels.** My life was instantly elevated. As a teenager, I did not know that space (i.e., a car) **plus** money would be my Golden Equation. I now see that I've repeatedly blended Money and Space.

- **My life in multiple cities/spaces:** I started this book in Seattle, WA, continued it in Richmond, VA and finished it in Mexico City and Tijuana. I travel to various spaces because I access the energy of the people and the land. Also, I know if I honor and protect my Space Currency while writing this book, then you, as the reader, will benefit from my North Star Currency alignment.

She became braver. She invited people to tell their bean counting stories. She asked about their numbers. She translated their words about decimals and commas into stories that were full of trauma, tears, celebration, pain, societal pressure, and even joy. And as she listened, she felt life flow through her—head to toe. She began to let her heart speak while her mind calculated costs, envisioned opportunities, and reimagined hope.

I am *more* at home with myself because The Currency Paradigm invites bigger imagination for what is possible. I hope you feel more at home too.

Welcome to a whole New World!
You made it.

Do you have more permission to live into currency flow?

Do you envision ways to traverse out of the fog?

Do you sense the warm wind at your back, the beaming sun on your face, the intuitive waves of your body's wisdom, and the earth beneath your feet?

If so, you are flying out of the hallucinatory fog, with The Magic Compass as your guide. Your North Star Currency is calibrated and pointed towards wholeness and integration. You feel the flow of a Cosmic Currency Figure Eight surrounding your existence!

TIME   ENERGY

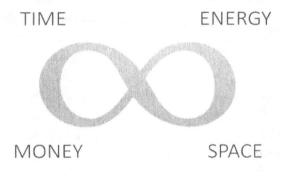

MONEY   SPACE

Welcome to this infinite space…

- A space to see clearly as you live fog free.
- A space to feel joy in your currency flow.
- A space to activate your primal and powerful imagination.
- A space to find more of YOURSELF!

You made it!

"You had the power all along the way, my dear. You just had to learn it for yourself."
Glinda, The Good Witch,
The Wizard of Oz (1939)

The Other Currencies

"The Other Currencies" is a poem written by Mollie Taylor.
Mollie wrote this poem after attending a workshop.
May we all imagine and live into a world with other currencies.

Imagine a life defined by more
than the flow of money or the passage
of time—also, the presence (or absence)
of energy and the opening (or closing)
of space.

A world unfurled that day, one
large enough, courageous enough
to proclaim the truth not many
are daring to speak: how we live
within the confines of a mono-currency
system and call it a life.

On the other side is a world
informed not merely by money,
but by the rhythmic flow
of energy, the expansive nature
of space, time shot through
with the glory of presence.

Can we quit fooling ourselves
and call consumerist culture what it is?

A fiction, a fable, fear—
written to inhibit, constrict, squeeze
out every ounce of delight, until
we collapse in a heap of dis-ease.

No, this is not a life.

It is fear.
It is fiction.
It is fable.

Let's at least have the courage
to call it what it is.

Mollie Taylor

To further explore *The Currency Paradigm* with thought-provoking questions and guided practices, visit:

www.thecurrencyparadigm.com

ABOUT THE AUTHOR

Hi! I'm Hillary.

Dream Doula. Financial Guide. Executive Coach.

I created and developed *The Currency Paradigm* because I longed for a place to foster imagination within a multi-currency universe. I love to cultivate new currency conversations in order to experience a spacious world of possibilities and vibrant ideas.

My services are often labeled *coaching* or *consulting*, but I consider my work like a walk, supporting others as they find their path toward a fuller way of being. I hope this book helps you travel near, far, deep, and wide, until you return home to yourself, feeling the miracle of being YOU.

www.hillaryaugustine.com
thecurrencyparadigm.com

Praise for *The Currency Paradigm*

In this powerful book, Hillary challenges a limited way of being and invites us into expansive territory to consider our own infinite potential with currency. Her inspiring and thoughtful storytelling summons the part of us that wants to join her to imagine outside the constrictions of scarcity and evolve into multidimensional beings who live in abundance across all spectrums of life. It is through her talents that we are gifted knowledge in this dimension which then opens the portal to deeper wisdom outside of space and time.

Jenae Kiehne,
MA, Bridging Psychotherapy and Plant Medicine

In these uncertain times, many of us are asking questions related to our identity, values and purpose. How do we spend our days? Hillary's wisdom in *The Currency Paradigm* provides us with a much needed and fresh perspective on this conversation. Her generous voice will invite you to creatively consider what matters most to you and how to build a life around it.

Jon DeWaal,
Founder, Liminal Guide

After reading and interacting with *The Currency Paradigm*, I am a much better leader of both my life and organization. This book opened my eyes to perceive decisions beyond money and time, clarifying multiple ways forward. If you need to move from scarcity thinking to abundance, this is a must read!

Dr. Lynne Ellis-Gray,
MSW, D. Leadership & Theology, Executive Coach

Hillary's work continues to guide and inspire me to discover and embrace ever greater levels of flow, connection, creativity, vision, and abundance in my personal, financial, and professional lives. *The Currency Paradigm* is an outgrowth of her considerable financial, emotional, creative, and synthesizing genius. In this paradigm, she offers many interesting and useful entry points from which to approach her unique and powerful vision. She treats each of the four currencies as an analytic and contemplative study in and of themselves. Her vision really bears its full fruit in the way that she weaves and integrates all the currencies into a seamless and coherent whole. There's something truthful, alive, and deeply hopeful about her work; I highly recommend it.

Jordan K. Wolfe,
LMHC, CGP

I have experienced the topic of money as weary and worn: everything that could possibly be said has already been talked about and written. Hillary, however, has changed my perspective, my mind, my beliefs, and even my practices. Through *The Currency Paradigm*, she invites a beautiful and creative conversation about money that is surprisingly innovative and expansive (and not a bit weary or worn). Within its pages, Hillary walks alongside as wise sage and dear friend; she ushers in a brand-new world of currency that is healed and whole.

Ronna Detrick,
M.Div., Spiritual Director/Coach and Writer

NOTES

Hanh, Thich Nhat. *Peace is Every Step: The Path of Mindfulness in Everyday Life*. Bantam Books, 1991. p. 95.

hooks, bell. *Feminism is for Everybody: Passionate Politics*. Pluto Press, 2000. p. 110. (bell hooks does not capitalize her name.)

Jones, Phil. "What is a paradigm? What is a paradigm shift?" *Excitant*, 5 Feb. 2018. par. 19, excitant.co.uk./what-is-a-paradigm-shift/. Accessed 4 March 2022.

Pearce, Joseph Chilton. "On Language Development: Imagination Is More Important Than Knowledge - Learning by Doing." *Pathways to Family Wellness*, No. 33, The International Chiropractic Pediatric Association, 2012, parts. 10-12, pathwaystofamilywellness.org/Family-Life/on-language-development-imagination-is-more-important-than-knowledge.html. Accessed 10 March 2022.

"Splitting (psychology)." *Wikipedia*, Wikimedia Foundation, 11 March 2022. https: //en.wikipedia.org/wiki/Splitting_(psychology).

Under the Tuscan Sun. Directed by Audrey Wells, performances by Diane Lane, Raoul Bova, Sandra Oh, Touchstone Pictures, 2003.

Wizard of Oz. Directed by Victor Fleming, performances by Judy Garland, Frank Morgan, Ray Bolger, Metro-Goldwyn-Mayer, 1939.

CPSIA information can be obtained
at www.ICGtesting.com
Printed in the USA
BVHW051449240123
656980BV00017B/995